Original title:
Between the Windowpanes

Copyright © 2025 Creative Arts Management OÜ
All rights reserved.

Author: William Hawthorne
ISBN HARDBACK: 978-1-80587-119-4
ISBN PAPERBACK: 978-1-80587-589-5

Enigmas in Transparency

Through clear glass, a world unfolds,
With cats in hats and tales retold.
A squirrel dances with a flair,
While neighbors argue, unaware.

A bird in sunglasses shrieks with glee,
Bobbing to tunes from a distant spree.
A dog with a monocle takes a stand,
In a debate on who's the best in the land.

Narratives in Haze

Foggy views, a wobbly sight,
Mice on scooters zooming bright.
The baker juggles his flour with grace,
While juggling eggs fly all over the place.

A sneeze from a ghost, what a show!
As the milkman slips in his own flow.
Laughter erupts from a puff of steam,
In a world full of whimsy, it seems like a dream.

The Eye of the Beholder

Peeking out, my neighbor's a spy,
With binoculars set on a pie in the sky.
Who knew that dessert could cause such fuss?
With a beagle plotting, they'll make a big plus.

A cyclist draped in toilet paper rolls,
Turns heads while dodging a duck's tiny shoals.
Is that a fashion statement or just a mistake?
Either way, it's a sight to awake!

Shades of Solitude

Through tinted glass, the world can't peek,
Socks on cats whisper secrets to freak.
A goldfish debates with the armchair's fate,
While dreaming of oceans where it can skate.

A potted plant gives love advice,
To a cactus hoping for a good slice.
Within these shades, humor entwines,
In quirky stories where laughter shines.

Illusions at Dusk

A squirrel wears goggles, thinks he's a pilot,
While shadows dance, creating a riot.
Cats whisper secrets, they're plotting confetti,
As the mailbox winks, feeling all jetty.

The moon, in pajamas, chuckles so bright,
As crickets create music, bringing delight.
A world full of laughter, a whimsical spree,
At dusk, the absurdity, oh can't you see?

The Space Beyond

A shoe on the roof dreams of flight,
While spoons gossip slowly, oh what a sight!
The dog spies a fairy, who's lost her way,
In the middle of traffic, mid-leap, she'll sway.

A cactus in slippers gives it a go,
As the toaster burns toast, putting on a show.
The clock ticks in laughter, not worried at all,
For time is just humor, and humor is tall.

Fragments of a Day

A pancake is flipping, but won't hit the pan,
While the curtains are bowing to the teapot's plan.
The cat plays the piano, a real feline star,
While the fish in a bowl hums, "We've come far!"

The sun wears a hat made of popcorn delight,
While raindrops are giggling, drumming through night.
A misfit brigade, of socks and of socks,
Laughing at Mondays, oh how time mocks!

Breaths of Untold Stories

A lamp starts to narrate, tales from the dark,
As the fridge joins in, with a cool little spark.
A broom rides the winds like it's out on a date,
While shadows just chuckle, enjoying their fate.

The chairs tell of gossip from all kinds of folks,
While spoons swirl in circles, playing like hoax.
Each laugh holds a shimmer, each giggle a spark,
In this world of the silly, there's always a mark.

Colors of Contemplation

A yellow cat sprawls on the ledge,
With dreams of fish and a garlic wedge.
Chirping birds form a noisy band,
While squirrels plot as they munch on sand.

A parrot squawks with a cheeky cheer,
"Who needs a job when you've got a beer?"
The world spins on, but we just stare,
At odd-shaped clouds like they really care.

Framed in Stillness

The curtains flutter like a dance,
As neighbors quesiton that prancing glance.
A puppy barks at nothing much,
While I knock twice and play a hunch.

A ladybug sits, round as a dime,
Contemplating the meaning of rhyme.
Outside, a kid rides his bike too fast,
Screaming, "Look, Mom! I'm a superhero at last!"

Secrets of the Sill

Dust bunnies gather like old friends,
Sharing stories that never end.
A lone tomato plant stands so proud,
While I check my phone for a text from a cloud.

Wind whispers secrets through the glass,
Of losses and wins in a flippant class.
The plants lean in, eager to hear,
What juice today's got hiding near.

The Light Beneath

Sunlight dances, a playful tease,
Chasing dust motes, with such a breeze.
An old sock drops from the window frame,
No one claims it, but it's still a game.

Rain clouds gather, a moody crew,
They sip their tea, "What shall we do?"
Lightning giggles, "Let's create some fuss!"
And with a zap, they steal our bus!

Silent Conversations

The cat sits high, a regal queen,
With eyes that sparkle, but what does she mean?
I swear she rolls those eyes at me,
Like I'm the comic of her grand marquee.

A bird flits by, it claims its space,
Making faces, it's such a disgrace!
I laugh at their chatter, a silly oration,
Their pecking and purring, a grand presentation.

Views of the Heart

My neighbor's antics make my heart leap,
As he wrestles a chair that's a bit too steep.
He nods to his plants, so wise and grand,
While Mr. Squirrel shakes his tiny hand.

Peering out from my cozy nook,
I spy on the world, like a sneaky book.
Laughter erupts from every side,
What a joy to take such a wide-eyed ride!

Nature's Quiet Curtain

Rain taps soft on the shiny glass,
While the robins gossip as they pass.
In pajamas, I sip my afternoon tea,
Wondering how silly my life can be.

The trees are dancing, they look so spry,
As if they're laughing, oh my, oh my!
Leaves shake hands like old pals do,
Nature's giggles drift through my view.

Threads of Life Untangled

Life's a yarn that twists and twirls,
With dogs on leashes and little girls.
A game of hopscotch erupts by the gate,
As parents complain, "Why can't they wait?"

I peek at the chaos with glee in my heart,
Their laughter's the best kind of art.
Each thread's a story that keeps us alive,
What a comedy show—how we all thrive!

Light's Soft Embrace

Sunlight spills across the floor,
Tickling toes that seek to soar.
Cat sprawls wide, a living beam,
Dreaming dreams that chase a dream.

Moths dance in a ballet flurry,
While dogs drift, lost in their hurry.
The shadows joke as hours fly,
While birds gossip way up high.

Giggling light through panes does creep,
While sleepy plants begin to peep.
Everything's bright, yet soft and warm,
As laughter paints a friendly charm.

Here we sit, with tea in hand,
While the day slips like grains of sand.
Whispers of joy in each sunbeam,
Life's a funny, fleeting dream.

Faint Traces of Memory

Old photographs with corners frayed,
Tell stories of the games we played.
A laugh, a cry, a silly pose,
Our youthful folly still overflows.

The fridge hums nonchalant and wise,
As snacks await our hungry sighs.
A glimpse of us through frosted glass,
Dancing like future's timeless past.

Each memory's a quirky scene,
Lost socks, and cake with too much cream.
A treasured song that makes us grin,
Echoes of moments crammed within.

With giggles, we recall those days,
When life felt like a silly maze.
Each glance stirs joy, a humorous spark,
Faint traces left, igniting the dark.

A Passage of Time

Clock ticks loud, a sneaky thief,
Stealing seconds, but brings relief.
Tea gets cold while we muse and chat,
Time flows as slow as a sleepy cat.

Tick-tock's rhythm hums our song,
Yet we laugh, we can't be wrong.
Each hour slips with playful grace,
A race with space, we find our place.

Sunsets greet us with a grin,
As day surrenders to the din.
They whisper secrets behind the dusk,
In that soft blink, we find our trust.

Life's parade is loud and bright,
Yet in the chaos, we find our light.
Tomorrow's ghost, with smiles so kind,
Leaves traces of joy, intertwined.

Fables of Forgotten Moments

Beneath the clouds, the stories hide,
Of all the giggles, laughter wide.
Chasing shadows, we always find,
Fables of fun, gently entwined.

A splash from puddles, a wink from fate,
With a pop of gum, we feel so great.
Whispers of mischief dance in the air,
Funny little moments, simply rare.

The fridge holds mysteries, notes in jest,
Reminders of pranks, which one's the best?
Each corner hides a witty tale,
With heroes of laughter that never fail.

We gather like stars in a chandelier,
Recalling the gigs, a constant cheer.
Moments forgotten, now just a smile,
Creating fables that last a while.

Fractured Realities

Two squirrels dispute the last nut,
One's a master of playful strut.
The other's plotting, eyes all aglow,
Who knew brunch could spark such a show?

A cat on a fence, tail held high,
Judging the birds who dare to fly.
He dreams of a leap, but fate's not kind,
So he settles for fluff and a nap entwined.

From the rain-streaked glass, two frogs sing,
Hoping for flies, it's a delightful fling.
Yet all they catch is a passing breeze,
Oh, life's little mishaps bring such glee!

Outside, a dog chases its own tail,
Round and round, a comical trail.
While in his mind, he's chasing a dream,
In reality, he's just chasing a scream!

Portraits of the Past

Old cat pictures hang on the wall,
One's in a hat, the other looks small.
Each frame a story, a wink from the past,
Who knew kittens could grow up so fast?

Grandma's quilt has stories to tell,
Stitched with laughter, all turned out well.
Yet tucked in a corner, a sock on the side,
How many rogues have tried to hide?

The toaster pops up a slice of bread,
In a kitchen where breakfasts are dread.
But crumbs on the floor start to dance and prance,
Even the kitchen has its own chance!

Photos of family all piled high,
Each makes you laugh, oh my, oh my!
We all look a bit goofy, it seems,
Guess our youth was just full of dreams!

Quiet Observations

In stillness lies the art of peeking,
A curious cat, quietly sneaking.
On the porch, an old man reads the news,
While his glasses slip down, just for a ruse.

The wind carries whispers of two teasing crows,
Debating on snacks from last night's prose.
With a plop and a flap, their antics begin,
It's a circus today, oh what a win!

A leaf falls like a clumsy ballet,
Dancing with grace, then gone on its way.
While ants on a mission march on the floor,
I wonder if they ever stop to explore?

From this window, the world seems strange,
With distant laughter and dogs that range.
Yet in each moment of quiet delight,
Life's unpolished moments shine bright.

The World on the Other Side

Out there, a chicken dons a cap,
Holding court in an urban map.
With a cluck it struts, full of pride,
Who knew hens could enjoy the ride?

A dog in sunglasses basks in the sun,
Giving high-fives, oh it's all in good fun!
Watch as the world spins and whirls,
While he dreams of chasing golden curls.

In a garden, gnomes take a pose,
Waving their shovels, striking a close.
Each flower's a witness, giggling soft,
As their secret plans go aloft.

All from the glass, the oddities play,
Where mischief makes sure to stay.
In laughter and cheer, surprises unfold,
The other side shines with stories untold!

The Glassy Veil

A bird pecks softly at the glass,
Trying to enter, but alas!
I laugh as it bounces back in surprise,
As if it's met a wall in disguise.

Sunlight dances on the pane,
With shadows playing a funny game.
I wave and pretend to be in a race,
The sun's bright smile makes a silly face.

Raindrops race, who'll hit the ground?
I cheer for the slow ones, round and round.
They splatter, giggle, slide, and flop,
In this clear maze, they never stop.

A fly buzzes, plotting its flight,
But smacks the glass and gets a fright.
I chuckle at its tiny dance,
In a world where bugs take a chance.

Hidden Stories in Light

In sunny spots, the dust does twirl,
Each speck a tale, a secret swirl.
I wink at shadows under the sun,
As if they're hiding, just for fun.

The sun pours in, a liquid gold,
While I sit wrapped in stories untold.
The cat stretches, dreams on the sill,
In this cozy nook, time seems to still.

I spot a face in the cloudy wisp,
It smiles back with a playful lisp.
I wonder if it knows my name,
Or wants to join in this silly game.

The light shifts, creating a dance,
While I give dust bunnies a glance.
Oh, what a hoot, to see them prance,
Holding their breath as they dare to chance!

The Haze of Memory

With edges soft, like dreams half-told,
The past echoes in shades of gold.
I peer through misty thoughts now clear,
Finding laughter mixed with cheer.

Old photos fade, but laughter stays,
Like a cat caught in a sunlit blaze.
I giggle at how we used to play,
In our own silly, twisty way.

Nostalgia sits on the ledge outside,
Waving, playing, like a friend with pride.
I toast to memories, a silly toast,
To moments I cherished the most.

The past's a haze, with colors bright,
Dancing with whimsy, pure delight.
I lean closer, try to see,
How reflections shape which eyes will be.

A Whispered Reply

In the stillness, I hear a chat,
Between the curtains where shadows sat.
A whisper floats by, light and spry,
"Did you see that squirrel? Oh my!"

The wind giggles, rustles the leaves,
Telling secrets and silly reprieves.
I smile back at its subtle tease,
As it stirs up the memory breeze.

Outside, the world spins round and round,
While I stay still, barely a sound.
I nod to the clouds, a sly little grin,
For they know the fun that lives within.

The sun takes a bow, its day complete,
As darkness arrives in a sneaky sheet.
I whisper a joke to the stars above,
In this glassy world, it's all about love.

Reflections in Glass

Peering through the shiny glare,
A squirrel does a double dare.
It poses, strikes a silly stance,
While I giggle at its dance.

Two birds squawk like they plan a heist,
A worm looks panicked, and quite spliced.
Chirping gossip, oh so loud,
As we both chuckle with the crowd.

Prism of Secrets

Colorful hues bounce around,
A cat watches, the king uncrowned.
He swats at rainbows on the floor,
As laughter echoes through the door.

A glass of juice, it winks at me,
Like it's hiding secrets, oh so free.
But in this light, it comes alive,
It quips and jests, it seems to thrive.

Whispering Shadows

Shadows play tricks, sneaky and sly,
They twist and churn, trying to lie.
A ghostly finger points and tugs,
While I laugh at these playful jugs.

The curtains sway like they know a joke,
With every breeze, they gently poke.
Laughter dances in the air,
In this house of shadows, fun is rare.

Veils of Light

Soft beams filtering, making me squint,
A prankster sun, with a little glint.
It tickles my forehead, then it's shy,
Making me laugh when it makes me cry.

The dust motes whirl like tiny sprites,
Dancing and twirling, oh what delights!
They gather around like they're in a race,
Life's tiny jesters in this bright space.

Echoes of the Rain

Raindrops tap a merry tune,
Dancing on the cheeky moon.
Puddles whisper silly tales,
Of rubber ducks and playful gales.

Clouds in socks, a playful sight,
Making mischief with delight.
Splashing laughter all around,
As the world spins round and round.

Thunder grumbles, jokes it shares,
With lightning flashing funny stares.
Umbrellas twirl like fairground rides,
While raindrops slip on grassy slides.

Each storm's a party, unconfined,
With nature's giggles intertwined.
So let it pour, let's sing and sway,
In the playful rain, we'll laugh away!

Fragments of Distant Dreams

Chasing clouds on silver trails,
While a snail narrates tall tales.
Sleepy heads with snores so grand,
Scatter dreams across the land.

Giraffes play chess in the skies,
Unicorns sip tea, what a surprise!
Every star's a wink, they claim,
And sprinkle giggles like a game.

Whimsical birds in tiny hats,
Sing of tangled tales and spat.
With echoes from the vibrant past,
We'll find joy that forever lasts.

So let's skip stones of silly schemes,
And dance upon these distant dreams.
For every laugh a wish we spin,
In the realm where fun begins!

Shadows in Transparency

Shadows play hide and seek today,
They tickle toes and dance away.
A cat in shades, so cool, so sly,
Winks and twirls as clouds float by.

The sun slips on a banana peel,
Creating giggles that make us squeal.
While sillhouettes of trees have fun,
Casting jokes beneath the sun.

Transparent jokes, they float above,
Sprinkled with laughter, a dear love.
Each shadow tells a secret line,
Of funny fables, oh so fine.

In the light, we prance and prattle,
Tickling shadows that like to battle.
In this dance of sunny bliss,
We find the humor that we miss!

Gazing Through Stillness

Stillness speaks in funny tones,
As frogs croak to their silly phones.
A breeze whispers knock-knock delights,
While dust bunnies spin and take flight.

In the silence, popcorn pops,
As giggles echo from the rooftops.
Butterflies play tag with the air,
Each moment wrapped in laughter's care.

Time pauses for a cheeky grin,
As laughter bubbles deep within.
In quietude, mischief takes chance,
To dance and twirl in this still dance.

Gazing through a wink of glee,
We capture joy, as wild as can be.
So hold your breath, watch the fun bloom,
In the stillness, let laughter loom!

Echoes of the Outside

Raindrops tap like tiny feet,
Birds in the trees whistle a beat.
Squirrels racing, tails like a flag,
Neighbors arguing, their voices drag.

A cat watches, tail twitching fast,
While dogs bark loud, it's quite a blast.
An ice cream truck jingles on by,
Kids run out like it's a pie in the sky.

Someone mows the lawn with a grin,
While a child makes a mess with some spin.
The breeze carries laughter, it's light,
In this parade of pure delight.

Sunshine flickers through leafy sways,
Turning a lazy afternoon to plays.
Life dances outside, funny and loud,
All in a world that's vibrant and proud.

Woven in Transparency

A spider in the corner spins a web,
While I sip tea, feeling quite fab.
Dandelions play, blowing seeds in the air,
As I tap my fingers without a care.

A bird tries to sneak in through a crack,
I laugh at its antics—oh, what a knack!
A paper plane flies past my sight,
It crashes down, what a comical fright!

The wind whispers jokes, swirling around,
I giggle at clouds that tumble and bound.
Nature's humor is sharp and sweet,
In this moment, I feel so complete.

Through panes so clear, I watch the parade,
Life's funny moments, never to fade.
Each frame a picture, a snapshot of glee,
In this silly world, forever I'll be.

Silhouettes and Sunbeams

Sunbeams dance as shadows leap,
A cat yawns wide, then falls in deep.
A tree whispers secrets to the grass,
While I chuckle, as the squirrels pass.

The mailman slips, oh what a sight!
Packages tumble, an unplanned flight.
Laughter erupts from the window team,
As friends share tales that burst like cream.

Clouds meander, shaping silly forms,
A dragon here, a duck there storms.
Children cheer, a kite in the sky,
Chasing giggles, oh my, oh my!

In this dance of light, all troubles fade,
Everything's funny, nothing dismayed.
A world painted bright, where shadows play,
Together we laugh, in the sun's warm sway.

The Quiet Divide

Two neighbors argue, loud and clear,
Over whose lawn is more sincere.
While I sip coffee, barely awake,
Their epic duel, a hilarious mistake.

A bird lands right in their ruckus,
Chirping cheerfully, what good luck!
It hops along, pecking at ground,
As the neighbors' voices twirl around.

The cat spies on the baffling scene,
With a wink, it seems to intervene.
A dog joins in, barking with glee,
Creating a ruckus, oh what a spree!

Life unfolds in a funny way,
Through windows framed in a merry play.
Neighbors will bicker, it's all in good fun,
In the end, we all share the same sun.

Fragments of Longing

A cat prances past my sight,
With ribbons tied in full delight.
She leaps and spins, a graceful twirl,
In a world where dreams unfurl.

I sip my tea, it's quite the show,
As pigeons plot their next grand throw.
A dash for crumbs, they bob and weave,
Like life, it's silly, I must believe.

The sun's a wink; a gallant jester,
It paints the walls in hues, a fest-er.
I laugh aloud, the plants agree,
Life's quirks shine humorously.

So here I sit, a smile so wide,
Watching nonsense drift outside.
Oh, how I cherish this quaint parade,
Of silly whims a day has made.

The Spectrum of Hope

A squirrel steals my sandwich repast,
With nimble paws, it runs so fast.
It pauses just to wink at me,
As if it knows my sad decree.

Outside, the world in summer's glow,
A dancing bug puts on a show.
It twirls and spins with careless cheer,
While I just watch with a pint of beer.

Clouds parade like puffy sheep,
While dreams and thoughts begin to leap.
Each whisper from the breeze, a jest,
To lighten up this heart unrest.

Morning comes, with coffee fine,
I toast to life, that silly line.
For every chuckle, every giggle,
The joy, it feels like a warm wiggle.

Echoes Through the Glass

A bird with flair, a wild affair,
Sings notes of mischief through the air.
I clap along, a tune so bright,
It dances on the edge of night.

Frogs compete for croaky fame,
With goofy leaps, it's all a game.
While flowers nod as if to say,
'Embrace the silly every day!'

Rain drops down in friendly patter,
A tap-dance on my window platter.
I chuckle loud, the world arrayed,
With whimsy woven, truth conveyed.

Birds in formation, a silly flight,
They twist and twirl, a delight!
Here's to the laughter, short and sweet,
In echoes soft, life's silly beat.

Elusive Narratives

Behind the frame, a tale unfolds,
With quirks and twists that life beholds.
The neighbor's dog, a howling bard,
Wags its tail, living life hard.

A ladybugs' unexpected cheer,
Flaunts polka dots with haughty leer.
She sips the sunshine in full spree,
While ants march by with unity.

Mice trade secrets in the shade,
Spinning yarns that never fade.
The wind howls jokes from bygone days,
Weaving laughter in sunbeam rays.

I write it down in coffee stains,
A story spun from daily gains.
In every glance, a narrative's lease,
Life dresses up in humor's fleece.

Gazing Beyond the Rim

I saw a cat wearing a hat,
It pondered deeply on the mat.
A squirrel jogged, doing its best,
Claiming a nut was quite the quest.

Birds had a meeting, chirps in the air,
Plotting a scheme to catch the fair.
They'd steal a snack from the curious child,
Wings flapping wildly, they acted wild.

A dog in the yard was plotting a plan,
Dreaming of biscuits, oh what a span!
He scratched his head, then rolled in the dirt,
Next, he leapt up in his finest shirt.

The sun peeked in, a warm, silly grin,
Revealing the chaos where laughter begins.
Oh, what a world just outside my view,
Where laughter and mischief rendezvous!

Murmurs of the Outside

The grass whispers tales to the breeze,
Of ants in a line, moving with ease.
A frog in the pond croaks a bold claim,
That dragonflies fear his fanciful name.

Children chase shadows, a game they adore,
Tickling each other, they tumble on the floor.
A giggle escapes like a whiff of delight,
As they revel in chaos from morning till night.

A snail in a race, oh how it took time,
With dreams of a trophy that sparkled and shined.
The flowers were betting, the daisies stood tall,
But no one was ready for the quickest of all.

As echoes of laughter dance through the air,
I sit by the glass, enjoying the flare.
What antics abound just a glance away,
In the mirthful world where sweet jesters play!

Fractured Perspectives

Through the glass, a jester spins,
While pigeons plot and the mischief begins.
A mouse sent a postcard, I could tell,
From a friend at the bread shop, oh what a sell!

An owl in a tree, pretending to sleep,
Was actually keeping an eye on the sheep.
With a wink and a nod, it felt like a joke,
As the sheep counted dreams with their silly cloak.

The sun played peek-a-boo, a lighthearted show,
While shadows performed on the ground below.
What a circus, my view was so wide,
In this window of laughter, I take such pride.

Oh, the antics of nature, oh so sublime,
A riddle of chaos, all in good time.
With a chuckle and grin, I sit by my spot,
Thankful for mischief that laughter has brought!

Glimpse of the Outside

Just outside the frame, a dance unfolds,
A beetle with swagger, its story told.
With twirls and a twist, it catches my eye,
While daisies judge harshly, I can't tell why.

A jogger tripped over a gopher's bold hole,
Turns out the critter wanted the role.
With laughter unaided, they both took a bow,
Nature's own pranksters, oh look at them now!

The wind made a fuss, tousled a hair,
As clouds traded secrets, light as a flare.
A laugh echoed soft from the sky and the ground,
In this silly world, joy easily found.

I sip my tea, as the show dances on,
Delighted by chaos from dusk 'til dawn.
What wonders await in the bright and the chirpy,
A glimpse of sheer fun, oh isn't it purty?

Window to Tomorrow

The bird outside sings out loud,
A tune that makes me feel proud.
I wave at squirrels, they're so spry,
They flip and twist as they fly by.

The sun peeks in with a wink,
While I pretend to gently think.
With coffee stains on my best shirt,
I ponder why life's such a flirt.

The clouds parade, a fluffy sight,
They change their shapes, a silly flight.
I muse who painted the blue sky,
While birds go by with a quizzical cry.

A spider weaves its web so grand,
As I sip soup with a bread stand.
Tomorrow waits with a grin so sly,
Who knows what treasures lie nearby?

Shimmering Uncertainties

In a world where socks disappear,
I launch a search, wide and near.
Who knew my cat was a thief?
I chuckle softly, half in belief.

Through glass that's spotted with grime,
I spot a snail, oh what a climb!
He takes his time, he's not in haste,
A lesson learned, no need to race.

A shadow flickers on the wall,
Left by the postman, oh! What a call!
He leaves the mail, then spins around,
A dance of chaos, joy unbound.

The window holds a world so vast,
Where giggles and blunders are cast.
I tap the glass, say "hello" to fate,
And watch as life begins to skate.

The Gap Between Wishes

I tossed a coin, wished for a meal,
But all I got was a rubber wheel.
The neighbors laughed, I grinned back wide,
As my lunch danced with comedic pride.

A fly buzzes past with a royal flair,
I wonder if he has somewhere to dare.
He land on food, then takes to flight,
A daring stunt! What a funny sight!

Mice scurry by, they must be late,
For some cheese party, oh how great!
I open the window, give them a cheer,
While my sandwich disappears, oh dear!

A wish in a bottle, lost at sea,
Hoping for jelly—or maybe some brie.
Life's buffet is quirky and wild,
Filled with surprises that leave me beguiled.

Transient Connections

Every day, I wave to the trees,
They rustle back, with the breeze.
I swear they giggle, just like me,
In this odd little world, oh can't you see?

The flowers gossip in vibrant hues,
They share their secrets, their colorful views.
A bee buzzes by, a buzzing queen,
Sipping nectar, like she's on the scene.

I chat with shadows, they're quite profound,
Who knew that silence could be so sound?
They nod their heads, their wisdom flows,
In this strange realm where the laughter grows.

Connection is fleeting yet oddly grand,
Life's funny moments, we can all understand.
So I'll keep looking through my glass,
For joy in the moments that come to pass.

Whispers of the Breeze

The curtains dance, a playful tease,
While flies engage in mini-leas.
Outside, a dog fetches a tree,
As I sip tea, full of glee.

A squirrel scolds with wild delight,
Chasing shadows, oh what a sight!
The sun peeks in with a cheeky grin,
Inviting laughter, let the fun begin!

Breezy whispers spin tales anew,
Of sneaky cats and birds that flew.
I chuckle, stuck in my little nook,
As nature turns each page of the book.

From the sill, I spy a silly ant,
Marching on as if it can chant.
Oh, what a world caught in frolic bliss,
Through glassy views, adventures insist!

A World in Crystal

A raindrop races down the pane,
A tiny marathon, never in vain.
It wobbles, it sways, I start to cheer,
Who knew such thrills could come so near?

Reflections dance in puddles wide,
With splashes of color, they never hide.
Outside, a hat flies off a head,
While I laugh, cozied up in my bed.

Dirt-smeared puppies in playful chases,
Greet the day with mud-splattered faces.
The world outside, a funny show,
While I'm glued in, pretending to know.

Cracks in glass hold laughter tight,
As I sip cocoa, all feels right.
In this crystal world, oh what a sight,
Where giggles reign and hearts take flight!

The Silent Divide

From this perch high in the sky,
I witness the ants stampede by.
One stumbles, it causes a fuss,
While I giggle in my little bus.

A kid on a tricycle, oh what a show,
Pedaling fast, then moving slow.
He waves to birds, they take to air,
Thinking perhaps, it's all a fair.

The hedge grows wild, a fortress of green,
Where critters gather, a secret scene.
Each chirp and flutter brings a laugh,
As I watch this comedic half.

A neighbor yells, "Watch where you scooter!"
To a cat who thinks it's a hooter.
Oh, from my glass, the world's a play,
With comic twists that brighten the day!

Reflections of Solitude

In solitude, I watch and see,
A goldfish entertains with glee.
It swims in circles, avoids the gloom,
While I'm stuck in my sunny room.

Two pigeons quarrel over a crumb,
Each one thinks they're the only chum.
Their flappy wings, a funny dance,
I can't help but giggle at their chance!

Through the glass, the world's absurd,
Toe-tapping squirrels, the silliest herd.
One steals a nut, oh what gall!
As I marvel from this crystal wall.

The blend of quiet, jest, and cheer,
Paints my day, each moment near.
From my seat, a thrill unfolds,
In this silly space, joy never folds!

Lattice of Silence

A cat stares with eyes so wide,
At squirrels playing cat and hide.
A bird outside sings a punny tune,
While I sip coffee from a spoon.

The dandelions dance in a breeze,
Taunting kids up in the trees.
In my lap, a dog yawns loud,
As if to scorn this sleepy crowd.

A neighbor sneezes—it's quite the show,
The curtains twitch as if to go.
A tumbleweed rolls without a care,
Do they think we watch? Oh, we swear!

The sun dips low, painting a scene,
While kids skate past all dressed in green.
Through glass I giggle at their delight,
This silly view makes every night.

Veiled Intersections

The car honks loud as cats parade,
Around the street, in shades of jade.
A lady spills her grocery bag,
Chasing her cat that's gone a-drag!

A dog darts in with a floppy ear,
Wagging his tail, full of cheer.
Milk cartons float—a boat of dreams,
In puddles left from friendly streams.

An apple rolls down the sidewalk fast,
Chased by kids, they run at last!
Windowpanes frame this unclaimed race,
In laughter, they find the silliest place.

As twilight falls, skies start to sing,
Neighborhood watches all things swing.
Through veils of glass, the world's delight,
Turns each mundane, into a fright!

Journeys in the Frame

A snail creeps slow on the sill today,
I wonder if it has much to say?
An ant shows up—then two and three,
Planning a party? Oh, let it be!

A kite flies high with strings undone,
While I'm stuck here, not having fun.
That little girl squeals, 'It's a bird!'
I chuckle, thinking, "Not quite, nerd!"

The colors shift as day turns night,
In this frame, everything feels light.
A romance blooms with a rose in hand,
As lovers glance across the land.

A flash of light—oh, what a show!
Through the glass, a comical glow.
Journeys unfold in a simple glance,
Where laughter and joy lead the dance.

Sentinels of the Senses

A flower pot spills with sneaky roots,
Socks on lines flutter like festive hoots.
The mailman trips—what a silly sight,
Nothing like a job gone slight!

A toddler giggles, trying to climb,
"Look at me, Mom!" he sounds prime.
A bird gives him a knowing look,
As if to note he's mischief's rook.

The breeze carries whispers of delight,
Of neighbors sharing secrets at night.
I sigh at the tales told in hushed tones,
While my cat battens down his own thrones.

In the dim light, the world feels vast,
But joy floats by, it's here to last.
Through glassy sight, we keep the glee,
Sentinels guarding all, just see!

Chasing Fleeting Glances

I spy a cat on the sill,
With eyes like saucers, such a thrill!
The neighbor slips, a funny sight,
While I barely stifle my delight.

Birds mock the dog, they tease and taunt,
As he barks madly, legs all gaunt.
I laugh and munch on a cookie treat,
The crumbs fall, oh what a feat!

A squirrel darts past, a feathered fuss,
Chasing its tail, oh what a plus!
Laughter erupts, as they tumble down,
A whirlwind of antics in this sleepy town.

Yet through these panes, each giggle stays,
Like little raindrops on sunny days.
Moments fleeting, like shadows they dance,
A funny tale in a single glance.

The Breath of Daylight

Sunlight peeks around the blinds,
A race of shadows it unwinds.
The dog yawns first, then shakes his fur,
As I sip coffee, feeling a stir.

The lawn gnomes watch with cheeky grins,
As a squirrel plots its next silly spins.
A swimmer's pose, all arms and legs,
But ends up tangled like broken pegs.

I wave to neighbors wearing capes,
While cats play cards, in all their shapes.
Life's a jigsaw of odd views,
Where laughter erupts from morning blues.

Bright pictures painted with cheerful strokes,
Daily antics, oh the silly jokes!
Daylight breathes, igniting a cheer,
As I savor coffee, so rich and clear.

Paths Untraveled

Two feet wander down the lane,
With mismatched socks, they're slightly insane!
A dog with shades and a flowered hat,
Chasing after a very loose cat.

Puddles reflect all the worlds they've seen,
Dancers in wellies, oh what a scene!
With each step taken, the laughter grows,
A true comedy, where anything goes.

The trees stand tall, pretending to sway,
As we invent our own silly play.
A movie without script or frame,
Just giggles and joy, what a wild claim!

Paths untraveled, a dance so free,
Full of whimsy for you and me.
Every step bright with a touch of jest,
Oh, the fun that life can manifest!

A Canvas of Fading Memories

Once a crayon, bright and bold,
Now it sits in shadows, old.
Sketches of laughter fade like mist,
Yet dreams begin with a playful twist.

A canvas filled with silly schemes,
In wacky colors, bright with dreams.
Each squiggle tells a funny lore,
A pop of laughter, forevermore.

Ghosts of giggles cling to the air,
As time slips by without a care.
With every stroke, I begin to see,
The joy of what's still yet to be.

A splash of joy, and oh, what fun!
Memories captured, never done.
In every line, a story grows,
A tapestry woven where laughter flows.

The Unseen Passage

A cat in a hat, what a sight to see,
Peeking at pigeons, oh so carefree.
The world outside dances, so far away,
While socks on the lawn play hide and sway.

A dog in a tutu, struts on by,
Chasing its tail, oh my oh my!
Neighbors all chuckle, they can't help but stare,
As bubbles float past, with nary a care.

An old man with glasses, a spy on his chair,
Counts all the squirrels, with extensive flair.
I swear one's wearing a shiny new shoe,
As laughter erupts from the invisible crew.

A crow takes a bow, it's a true diva,
While squirrels plan heists, they're quite the achievers.
Through ghostly reflections, the antics unfold,
Life's funny ballet, a sight to behold.

Colors Beyond the Frame

Yellow dance shoes on a green-painted fence,
Frogs sing in harmony, truly immense.
A rainbow of socks, all mismatched in cheer,
Lean out for a better view, can you hear?

Butterflies drag race, oh look, it's a sprint!
While ants on a mission carry crumbs – what a hint!
Giggles burst forth from a bush by the door,
As a squirrel gets stuck in a tangle of lore.

An elephant chuckles, it's riding a bike,
While geese form a band, all honking alike.
A parade of oddities shakes up the scene,
Where laughter and colors merge in between.

From cerulean skies to a violet shade,
Life's silly escapades in grand masquerade.
With chortles and murmurs that rise with the breeze,
Is it a dream, or just whims in the trees?

Faded Glances

A snail on a skateboard, what a fine treat,
Zooming quite slowly, with snail-magic feet.
The flowers all giggle as clouds drift on by,
Underneath an umbrella, a frog says, "Oh my!"

A raccoon with a monocle reads from a tome,
While critters on bicycles roam far from home.
They stumble on jam, a sticky surprise,
And laughter erupts under leafy disguise.

A bear in a bowtie admires the scene,
As squirrels host tea parties, quite serene.
Through the blurred memories of what seems so clear,
The cheer in their antics brings a smile and a cheer.

Time flickers and fades like the dusk's lazy grace,
In this comical dance, we all find our place.
So peek through the frames where the humor resides,
And relish each moment as joy swiftly glides.

The Barrier of Senses

A window's a canvas, where laughter is drawn,
With fingers on glass, the silly's not gone.
The butter on toast does a wobbly jig,
While pancakes do salsa, all set for a gig.

A chicken in slippers navigates the street,
As ducks in a line simply can't find their beat.
The sights and the sounds, a parade for the day,
Where mischief is king, and the jesters do play.

Oh, the smell of fresh cookies leads cats on the chase,
As shadows play tag in this whimsical space.
A tap dance by crickets, a light-hearted show,
While fireflies join in with a soft, glowing glow.

Through all of the chaos, there's fun to be had,
As laughter cascades, and the moments feel glad.
There's joy in the distance, where senses collide,
In this comical world, let the giggles reside.

Journey of the In-Between

In a world where dust bunnies dance,
I ponder the day and my silly chance.
With an apple in hand, I dream about,
A journey where shadows wiggle about.

The cat on the sill looks rather confused,
As I sip my tea, feeling bemused.
What's outside? A parade of ants,
In tiny top hats, are they in a trance?

The postman arrives with a letter from Mars,
A postcard that says, 'We've sent you our stars.'
I chuckle and grin, the mailbox a stage,
For jokes of the cosmos, a comic's page.

With a wink to the clouds, I blow them a kiss,
Each drift like a joke that's too good to miss.
Through cloudy reflections, the laughter will ring,
In the space of the in-between, joy's the thing.

Mosaic of Reflections

A mirror of thoughts in the morning light,
Where squirrels play poker, oh what a sight!
With pancakes flying like fluffy dreams,
And syrup rivers that flow in sweet streams.

The toaster pops up, it's a surprise!
Burnt toast becomes art, oh how time flies.
I sip my coffee, a silly affair,
As blobs of cream do a dance in mid-air.

The goldfish swims in its bubble of glee,
Plotting a heist with a leaf and a pea.
Oh, what a banquet for fables to spin,
As I giggle softly at what could've been.

Around the clock, the antics unfold,
With laughter and chaos, like treasures of old.
Each moment a piece, a colorful scheme,
In the mosaic of life, where I dare to dream.

The Weave of Life's Tapestry

Threads tangled up in a quirky design,
As socks exchange tales over glasses of wine.
The needle's a waltzer, it hops to the beat,
In a fabric of giggles, life's little treat.

With each stitch a story, a pun or a jest,
The fabric comes alive, never more stressed.
Platypus dressed up for a grand masquerade,
While llamas wear hats from the thrift store parade.

Beneath the loom, the oddest sights bloom,
Like a cactus in clogs, you can't find in a room.
The warp and the weft, they play hand in hand,
Stitching up laughter across this wild land.

When life's loom is busy, and colors unite,
We weave all the nonsense into pure delight.
Each wacky adventure, a thread gone astray,
In the weave of our tales, we find joy every day.

Whispers Beyond the Glass

In a world where bugs dance, and shadows play,
My cat thinks the birds plot an escape each day.
Silly tales of what she sees all night,
Conversations with bugs, oh what a sight!

A squirrel in a tux, he's stealing the scene,
Dressed for a party, he's looking so keen.
I can't help but giggle, what a funny show,
Nature's own sitcom, with a perfect glow.

The raindrops gossip as they race down wide,
Each one a traveler, with secrets to hide.
They splash on the sill, like laughter out loud,
Mischief in droplets, the window's proud crowd.

Oh, the world's a play in this glassy frame,
Moments turned to jest, never quite the same.
Outside my fortress, the quirks take a hold,
With laughter on the breeze, green stories unfold.

A World Refracted

Through shards of sunlight, the colors explode,
A rainbow of nonsense, in laughter bestowed.
Butterflies in tutus, birds in bow ties,
A whimsical landscape of comic surprise.

Reflections are silly, and so is my hat,
A strange little echo, a dancing chitchat.
My dog thinks he's regal, prances about,
Together we chuckle, we laugh, and we pout.

The curtain of rain paints the world anew,
Each droplet reflects all the things we pursue.
A puddle becomes a pool of delight,
We jump in together, just follow the light.

With each silly shadow, a giggle takes flight,
In this refracted world, nothing's ever slight.
A merry adventure unfolds in the gleam,
Look close through the glass, and you'll see the dream!

Fleeting Moments Captured

A bird on the ledge with a camera to see,
Snapping quick glimpses of starlings so free.
Flashy and dapper in their feathery suits,
Candid moments captured, oh what a hoot!

My friend with a mug thinks he's a great chef,
Each sip a performance, a laugh 'til we're left.
The steam from his beverage beckons a cheer,
A fine cup of chuckles served weekly, I fear.

I spy with my eye, a worm wearing shades,
Sipping on dewdrops, in slick masquerades.
This fleeting parade, it offers delight,
In a world through the glass, where humor takes flight.

And here in this frame, a slice of the day,
Moments like this are the fun's grand buffet.
With each fleeting grin, life's secrets unfold,
In laughter and joy, the stories retold.

Light and Lamentations

A shadowy figure on the windowsill,
Wondering why the goldfish never stand still.
They swim in circles, a joke on replay,
While I sit and ponder, forgetting the day.

The sun makes a joke as it slips through the glass,
Hiding its warmth in a field of sweet brass.
I laugh at the curtains, they dance and they sway,
Curtains gossip daily in their soft ballet.

The moonlight tiptoes, a thief in the night,
Stealing my dreams and twisting them tight.
With luminous giggles, it plays hide and seek,
A luminous prank in a world so unique.

Yet laughter lingers, and shadows confess,
There's humor in life, even in a mess.
With light and lament, we embrace every whim,
Through glass that reflects all, our laughter won't dim.

Intricate Landscapes

The cat stalks the garden, it knows no fear,
Chasing after shadows that suddenly appear.
The dog on the porch, a king in the sun,
Watches all the chaos, oh, what fun!

A squirrel takes charge, with a dash and a leap,
While the birds on the wire gossip and peep.
The flowers in bloom, they wiggle and sway,
As if they're in on the joke of the day.

Bees buzzing loudly, in search of a snack,
But one fancies a ride on the snail's little back.
They laugh at the breeze, a tickling friend,
In this open-air circus, where wonders never end.

Under the sky, life's a comical scheme,
Every corner, a jest, every moment, a dream.
With giggles and grins all around in sight,
Nature's own theater, oh, what a delight!

Moments Caught in Time

A toddler with cake, in frosting she's drowned,
Mom's snap of the moment, oh look how she's crowned!
With a grin that's sticky and fingers that smudge,
Childhood's a party, it's hard not to judge.

Uncle's new glasses, perched high on his nose,
He looks quite the scholar, in terrible clothes.
As he reads the fine print, the dog steals the show,
His shoelace is tasty, oh no! What a foe!

Grandpa's tall tales, fish that got away,
Always growing bigger, day after day.
While Grandma just chuckles, she knows all the tricks,
And the fish is now larger than politics.

Each snapshot a giggle, a treasure in time,
Framed in the laughter, each memory a rhyme.
Life spins in circles, with joy that won't hide,
In moments caught laughing, how little we bide!

Gazing Through Barriers

Peering through curtains, the neighbor's a sight,
Dancing in pajamas, what a curious flight!
The cat on the windowsill snickers and winks,
While dreaming of tuna, and plotting mischief stinks.

A mime in the street, trapped in his box,
Mimicking movement, how he always shocks!
Yet no one around seems to bother at all,
As squirrels take bets on the mime's next fall.

The goldfish watches, with a giddy delight,
As a dog tries to howl at a cat in mid-flight.
Each glance through the glass, keeps the fun alive,
With antics so wild, only laughter can thrive.

Through barriers we chuckle, at life's little quirks,
Each moment a show, with no need for perks.
As laughter escapes, like bubbles that burst,
We peek through the barriers, and quench our great thirst!

Translucent Dreams

Behind frosted glass, where the odd shapes reside,
I glimpse a strange world, where imaginations glide.
A unicorn tiptoes, on clouds made of cream,
While fairies are painting their own brand of dream.

The giant, a baker, with cakes stacked so high,
Coughs up a rainbow from his oven nearby.
Chocolate raindrops, they splatter the floor,
As the gnomes try to catch them, who could want more?

A leprechaun juggles, with four-leafed delight,
While wind whispers secrets, all through the night.
No worries or cares, just giggles and glee,
In this translucent realm where we all want to be.

Through these whimsical visions, we laugh and we play,
As daylight bursts in, chasing dreams all away.
But memories linger, sweet as a dream,
In a world full of laughter, life's one funny theme!

Nature's Diaphragm

A squirrel in a sweater, so chic and spry,
Jumps from branch to branch, oh my, oh my!
It thinks it's a bird, all feathers and flight,
Yet it's just a chubby little fur ball in sight.

The flowers gossip, they whisper and sway,
"Did you see that squirrel dance just today?"
The bees laugh softly, their buzz quite a tease,
As they sip on nectar with calm, steady ease.

Clouds roll in, wearing hats made of cream,
The sun winks down, it's all quite a dream!
Nature giggles, a chorus so loud,
With squirrels and flowers, it's merry and proud.

So let's join the laughter, let's sing with a cheer,
Nature's the party, don't you want to steer?
With every rustle, a joke to be found,
In this wild, vibrant world, let's dance all around!

Shadows of Curiosity

A cat in the corner, with a tail like a plume,
Stalks the shadows, filling the room.
With curious eyes, it spies on the light,
Chasing its own tail is quite the delight!

The lamp stands tall, and it flickers a grin,
Casting odd shapes that give everyone spin.
A shadow of pie, a shadow of cheese,
Oh, look over there! A shadow of fleas!

A pup with a bounce joins the playful charade,
Bounding through darkness like a sunbeam parade.
They pirouette softly, with steps oh so spry,
While the old grandfather clock says, "Oh my, oh my!"

Curiosity dances in the glow of the night,
Chasing after jesters that slip from their sight.
With each little giggle, their shadows expand,
In this whimsical world, it's fun that is planned!

Glowing Edges

The moon beams softly, dressed in a robe,
Tickling the trees, marking every globe.
Fireflies twinkle, they sketch in the air,
Painting the darkness, without any care.

A hedgehog rolls past, all spines and no fright,
Stumbling right over a leapfrog parade.
"Are you lost?" croaks a frog, with a grin big and wide,
"Or just looking for trouble on this joyful ride?"

In the glow of the evening, laughter abounds,
As critters collide with the softest of sounds.
The stars start to twinkle like fish in the sea,
While crickets form bands that play tunes wild and free.

So here's to the night, with all its delight,
Where shadows and giggles take charming flight.
Glowing edges whisper, in the softest embrace,
In the heart of the night, we all find our place!

The Silent Observer

A mouse in a tux, what a sight to behold,
Watches the party, all timid and bold.
Nibbling on crumbs, it keeps a keen eye,
As the humans all dance and the cakes start to fly.

A turtle peeks out from its cozy small shell,
Curious about this loud, lively yell.
It wonders if parties have music like rain,
Or if it can join—should it waddle or strain?

The clock counts down, the snacks disappear,
And mice don tuxedos to dance with good cheer.
Each tiny step taking a beat from the band,
As the world starts to whirl in a dance so unplanned.

The silent observer chuckles with glee,
Watching the antics as wild as can be.
In this world of laughter, so grand and so bright,
Every creature can join in, on this whimsical night!

Fractured Reflections

I gaze at the glass, what do I see?
A squished little bug with a grumpy decree.
My hair's all a mess, like a bird took a flight,
Laughing at my look, oh what a silly sight!

The world on the other side's such a tease,
A squirrel wearing sunglasses, up in the trees.
But who would've thought, with this sunny display,
I'd swear it was winter, come what may!

As I sip my tea, the view starts to blur,
A raccoon doing ballet? Yup, that's quite a stir!
These scenes through the pane, absurd and absurd,
Make daylight a wonder, but silence my word!

I chuckle and grin, as I watch all the fun,
From inside my cocoon, in the warmth, I'm the one.
Who's laughing at what? The glass holds my jest,
In a world of reflections, I'm truly the best!

Light's Gentle Barrier

The sun casts a glow on the wall of my room,
It dances and jiggles, dispelling the gloom.
A feisty little shadow starts jiving around,
What a strange little party inside my compound!

My cat's at the window, with a paw up so high,
Looks like she's waving, 'I see you! Oh my!'
With a meow that's a giggle, she leaps for her prize,
Chasing beams of sunlight, what a clever surprise!

The mailman rolls by on a bicycle path,
Sprinkling confusion and a bit of a laugh.
"Is that a dog in a hat?" I say with a cheer,
Just light playing tricks in my cozy frontier!

Behind this soft veil, silliness reigns,
A world full of laughter, where joy still remains.
I'll stay with my shenanigans, til day's end,
With a giggle, a chuckle, and no need to pretend!

The Veil of Glass

I watch from my fortress, a palace of glass,
Where the world outside tales of wonder do pass.
A fox in a tux, holding paws, such a sight,
Fashion trends that have gone a bit too light!

A ladybug struts with its polka-dot charm,
Flirting with flowers, oh what a fine balm.
But wait! There's a squirrel, an acorn in tow,
Whispering secrets that only he knows!

I sip on my cocoa, it's sweet as can be,
Imagining dance-offs together they'd see.
A multitude of antics behind the clear wall,
In this stage of the world, I'm a watcher of all!

With each passing moment, laughter comes near,
Jokes told by shadows both stubborn and dear.
So here I will sit, with my humor held fast,
In the realm of the funny, where joy's never last!

Captured Outside

The world is a comedy show just on cue,
Two ducks in a row, painting the town blue.
While one struts with flair, the other gets shy,
Both wearing the finest of feathery ties!

A garden so lively, with tricks up its sleeve,
A gnome grinning wide, I just can't believe!
He's cracking a joke with a beetle so fat,
What a whimsical scene, oh imagine that!

The wind teases flowers, they giggle and sway,
As they dance hand in hand, in their colorful display.
Through the glossy interface, life's quirks come alive,
In this festival of farce, where fun seems to thrive!

So here I remain, in my humorous nook,
With laughter as my ally, and joy in my book.
The view through this veil is a canvas of cheer,
Captured in moments, forever held dear!

www.ingramcontent.com/pod-product-compliance
Lightning Source LLC
Chambersburg PA
CBHW070316120526
44590CB00017B/2704